A Walker's guide

by

Steve Burton
Max Maughan
Ian Quarrinton

**(Members of the Derby Group of
the Ramblers' Association)**

First published by
Thornhill Press
24 Moorend Road
Cheltenham

ISBN 0 904110 88 5

Printed by
R. J. Washington
Southwood Lane
Cheltenham
Glos

CONTENTS

Whilst every effort has been made to ensure the accuracy of information contained in this guide, neither the authors nor the publisher can accept responsibility for the consequences of any inaccuracies. All the tracks and paths shown are, to the best of knowledge, rights of way. Access Land on rare occasions may be closed. If in doubt check with the Peak Park Planning Board.

We would like to record grateful thanks to those who have helped us, in particular Phyllis Oldknow for typing the manuscript; English Sewing Ltd. and Severn Trent Water Authority for information concerning their establishments, and members of the Derbyshire Area Ramblers' Association for their advice and encouragement.

S.B.
M.J.M.
I.N.Q.

FOREWORD
by Phillip Whitehead, M.P.

It was in the lifetime of many ramblers who are still active that the struggle for access to the Derbyshire Peak began to be won. The Ramblers' Association has done much to bring home to the people of Derbyshire and visitors from far afield the heritage of history and landscape on our doorstep. This guide to the Gritstone Way is not only an appropriate reminder of Footpath Heritage Week in 1980; it also meets the need for a guide which will link town and country, peakland, city and dales, in a route which all can attempt, either in stages or as a whole.

Living as I do at Rowsley, the midway point of this route; I always regret how many people storm through the towns and villages of the Derwent Valley, in their eagerness to get to the real beauties of the northern hills and stately homes. This guide has a surer touch. It will lead the discerning walker through much of the past which has shaped us all, and more unexpected beauty, which too many of us see only through the haze of our exhaust fumes.

This guidebook will be read with pleasure, carried with profit, and retained with a sharp and lasting memory of the unexpected delights of the Gritstone Way. Some will want to refer to it on a passing visit where only a short walk is possible. Others I hope will set themselves a weekend or longer to do as much of the whole route as they can, diverting to the places of note along the way, until the moment comes for the last stage, the exhilerating climb up to Win Hill and then along the ridge to Mam Tor. When you do that you will understand why Lord Byron wrote that there are things in Derbyshire as beautiful as anything you will see in Switzerland. All there for the taking, on your own doorstep, free as the clean air you will be breathing.

INTRODUCTION

The concept of a continuous walking route along the gritstone from Derby to Edale was formulated by members of the Derbyshire Area Ramblers' Association in 1970.

As information on the route was very limited, Derby Group of the Ramblers' Association decided to resurvey the route and write a guide as their contribution to Footpath Heritage Week 1980. Problems such as new housing, broken footbridges, etc., have been encountered and the route now described circumvents the majority of these problems and offers the walker a very varied 56 miles.

Geologically Derbyshire consists mainly of two rock types, Carboniferous Limestone and Millstone Grit, both formed during the Carboniferous Period about 300 million years' ago. Soon after this, these rocks were uplifted and folded into a dome structure called an anticline, which, after erosion, exposed the limstone in the centre of the dome and the Millstone Grit along the sides. The latter consists of shales and coarse sandstones, and the sandstones, being more resistant, have weathered out to form upstanding scarps or "edges" running from north to south on the western and eastern sides of Derbyshire. It is along this series of eastern gritstone edges that the route of the Derbyshire Gritstone Way runs (hence its name).

Both Derby and Edale are easily accessible, rail and bus connections being available. The route lends itself to be walked in a variety of ways, depending on the walker's ability and personal preferences—either in easy stages, staying at hotels, guest houses or camping, by incorporating the route in a number of loops taking in adjoining countryside, or as a challenge walk, backpacking. Any person completing the walk in a single stage or consecutive stages is entitled to apply for a badge (the design is on the title page). Send brief details of route, details of your experiences, a S.A.E. and 80p (cheques and P.O. payable to Derby Group Ramblers' Association) to Max Maughan, 146 Vicarage Road, Mickleover, Derby.

REMEMBER that although the route described is on rights-of-way or Access Land, you are crossing private farmland or moors, and the Country Code should be observed.

MAP OF DERBY CITY CENTRE

Showing features of Interest and start of Walk

Scale: 1 inch = ¼ mile

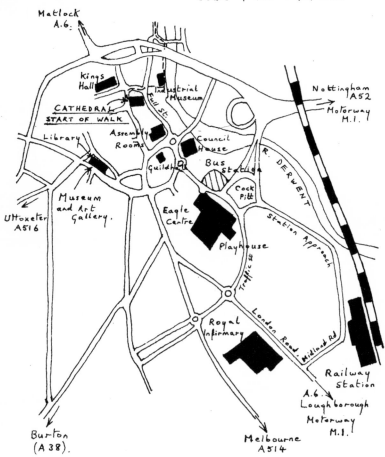

Crown Copyright Reserved

DERBY—BREADSALL

The walk begins in Derby. Excavations have revealed that settlements existed in Roman times by the River Derwent on the northern side of the present City Centre. There are traces of Saxon and Danish occupations, and by the Middle Ages a number of religious houses were established, including All Saints, now the Cathedral. The Industrial Revolution came early to Derby—John and Thomas Lombe's Silk Mill being erected in 1717. Other textile mills followed. Derby china works was founded in 1755 (becoming 'Royal Crown' in 1890).

THE CATHEDRAL, DERBY

THE SILK MILL, DERBY

The railways arrived in 1839, the latter providing the basic skills which led to Derby becoming a renowned centre for engineering. City status was bestowed in 1977.

Start at All Saints, Derby's Cathedral, the most striking feature of of which is the lofty 178 foot sixteenth century tower. The rest of the Cathedral was rebuilt by James Gibbs in the eighteenth century and contains a number of interesting sculptures. There is a fine example of Robert Bakewell's ironwork—a screen stretching the width of the building. Note also Bess of Hardwick's monument, an elaborate epitaph to a powerful and much married countess.

Make your way to the river, passing Derby Industrial Museum. The exhibits are housed in a building constructed in 1910 on the site of Lombe's original silk mill, which was gutted by fire. Some of the original foundation arches can be seen on the site facing the river. The exhibits include a collection of Rolls-Royce aero engines and displays illustrate Derbyshire's industrial development.

After passing under the Inner Ring Road, St. Mary's Bridge will be seen on your right. A bridge existed here in medieval times and a fine example of a Bridge Chapel still exists.

Walk towards St. Mary's Church in Bridge Gate but turn right, before reaching the church, along North Parade. Cross the route of a former railway line and proceed along Darley Grove.

Darley Abbey Village is soon reached. Take New Row down to the river and make for the Toll Bridge.

Darley Abbey was founded in the twelfth century as an Augustinian Priory. The main surviving structure has recently been converted into a public house. In 1783 Walter Evans established cotton mills on the opposite bank of the river. Houses were built around the abbey site to accommodate the workers.

Pass through the mill complex, taking the public footpath on the left, and follow the river northwards for about half-a-mile. Bear right over the railway and continue up the bridleway to the junction of the A61 and Croft Lane. Walk up Croft Lane to Breadsall Village. The church here has a fine fourteenth century steeple which is a prominent landmark.

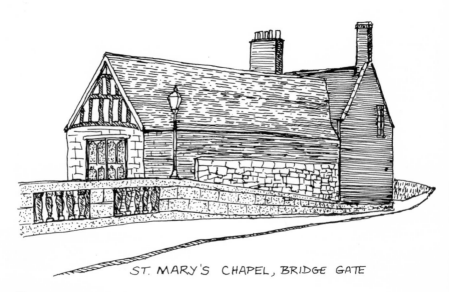

ST. MARY'S CHAPEL, BRIDGE GATE

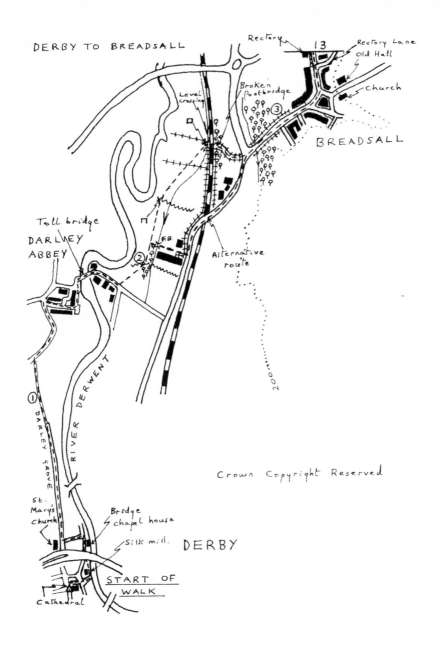

DERBY TO BREADSALL

Rectory

13

Rectory Lane
Old Hall

Church

BREADSALL

Broken
Footbridge

Level
crossing

③

Toll bridge
DARLEY
ABBEY

②

Alternative
route

FB

200

RIVER DERWENT

DARLEY GROVE

①

St.
Mary's
Church

Bridge
Chapel house

Silk mill.

DERBY

Cathedral

START OF
WALK

BRICK ROW, DARLEY ABBEY

BREADSALL CHURCH

BREADSALL—EATON PARK WOOD

Leave Breadsall by Rectory Lane. The route takes you past a waterworks and under the A38 dual carriageway, entering Little Eaton in Alfreton Road. The village lies on a spur of the former Derby Canal which served local paper mills. Some remains of the wharf may still be seen. Continue through the village over the railway bridge and take the footpath leading off Barley Close. At the top of the hill cross the field and turn northwards before reaching Park Farm. The footpath continues for half-a-mile to Eaton Park Wood.

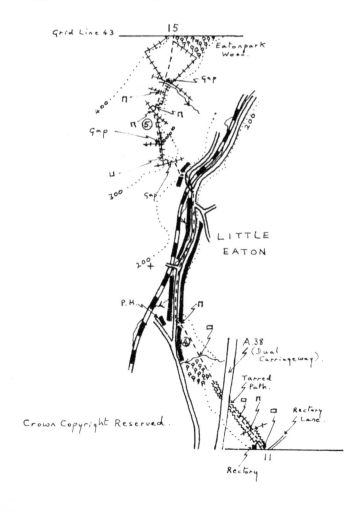

BREADSALL TO EATONPARK WOOD.

13

EATON PARK WOOD—MILFORD

Continue to Holbrook, crossing the line of the Derwent Aqueduct. This aqueduct is an arterial route for water supplies to South Derbyshire, Leicester and Nottingham. The sources are the Derwent Valley reservoirs which lie in the High Peak between Glossop and Sheffield. These reservoirs are fed, either naturally or by diversion from adjoining catchments, by the Rivers Derwent, Ashop, Alport and Noe. Water from the reservoirs is first treated and then fed into the aqueduct— a system of steel or cast iron pipes up to 48 inches in diameter. The green iron gates you will see from time to time on field boundaries lie above the pipelines and allow access for inspection and repair purposes.

In the village turn left up Mellors Lane, thence via a footpath to Makeney. Follow the road to Milford, crossing the River Derwent. Notice the entrance to the cotton mill where a bell is displayed. The inscription on the bell reads—"Wm. Chapman of London, Fecit 1781." It is thought that the bell was originally housed in one of the older Strutt mills at Nottingham or Milford and then transferred to the cruciform fireproof warehouse at Milford. The latter was built by Strutt in 1792 and stood on the opposite side of the main road to the present mill. It was demolished in 1964.

GEORGE STEPHENSON'S SIGHTING TOWER, CHEVIN

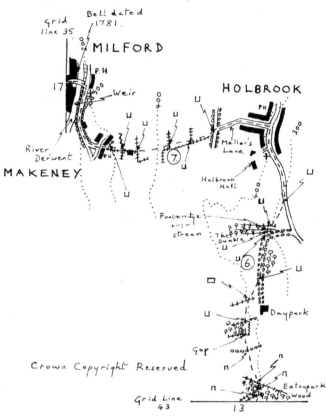

MILFORD, BELL FROM DEMOLISHED MILL

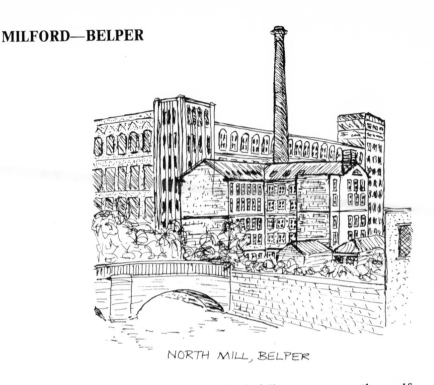

NORTH MILL, BELPER

Walk up Sunny Hill and along the bridleway across the golf course. The square gritstone tower on the right is a sighting tower built by George Stephenson during the construction of the railway tunnel in 1839.

Follow the bridleway across the Chevin, where fine views may be had of Belper. In the distance Crich Stand may be seen. This is a memorial to the Sherwood Foresters and stands on a limestone quarry edge. Crich is also the home of a Tramway Museum open to the public during the summer.

Just before the bridleway makes a sharp left turn to Farnah Green, take the footpath to the right down the hill and join Chevin Road for 100 yards. Then take footpath in front of Swiss House, which leads down to the river. Continue along the water meadows to Belper Bridge.

Crossing the bridge one passes the mill complex of English Sewing Limited. The oldest remaining structure is the North Mill of 1804. This was established by Jedediah Strutt and Richard Arkwright, whose other mills in Belper have since been demolished. The early mill buildings are now dwarfed by the seven-storey redbrick East Mill of 1912.

MILFORD TO BELPER.

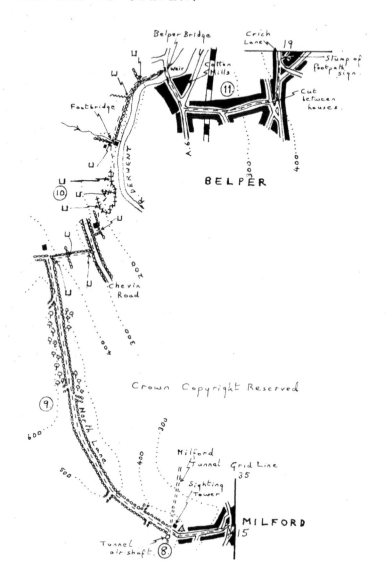

BELPER—RIDGEWAY

Walk up Long Row, past the industrial housing of the 1790s and leave Belper by Crich Lane.

Just past the junction with Marsh Lane take a footpath to the right and continue northwards past new houses and then over fields to Nether Heage. From here Dungeley Hill windmill can be seen. Recently restored, this is a good example of a tower mill with six sails.

Turn left at the end of Malt House Lane, passing on your right a house with an early Norwich Union Fire Insurance plate. Take the path across the fields to Ridgeway.

WINDMILL NEAR NETHER HEAGE

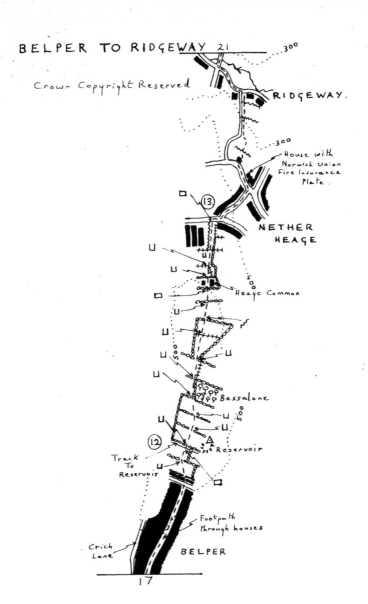

BELPER TO RIDGEWAY 21 ⸻ ...300

RIDGEWAY.

...300

House with
Norwich Union
Fire Insurance
Plate.

⑬

NETHER
HEAGE

U

U

U

Heage Common

U

U

U

U

Bessalone

U

U

U

U

⑫

△ Reservoir

Track
To
Reservoir

U

Footpath
Through houses

Crich
Lane

BELPER

17

RIDGEWAY—WHATSTANDWELL

Proceed on towards Bullbridge. At the main road, turn left, under the railway bridge. Cross the river and continue up the hill to the canal bridge. Take the canal tow path on the left.

Continue past the dyeworks and the gas plant—the footpath follows the boundary fences. You will pass traces of Stephenson's incline built in 1842 to connect lime quarries at Crich with kilns in Ambergate. The system operated by gravity, the descending full wagons being counter-balanced by raising empty ones.

Soon the Cromford Canal is reached and the route now follows the tow path to Whatstandwell.

CRICH STAND

RIDGEWAY TO WHATSTANDWELL

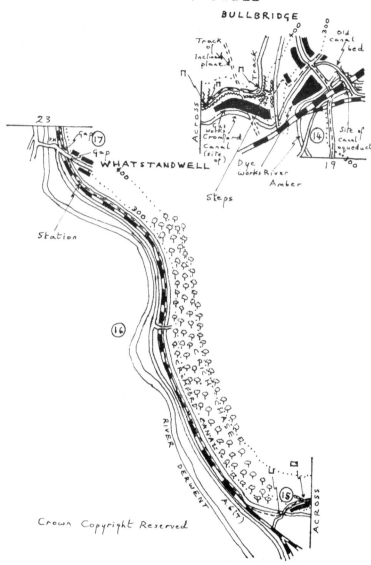

BULLBRIDGE

Track of Inclined plane

Track

Old canal bed

300

400

300

Across

works Cromford Canal (site of)

(14)

Site of canal aqueduct

19

300

Dye works River Amber

Steps

23

Gap (17)

Gap

WHATSTANDWELL

400

Station

300

(16)

River DERWENT

CANAL A(17)

(15)

Across

WHATSTANDWELL—BILBERRY KNOLL

Continue along the towpath to High Peak Junction where the line of the old Cromford and High Peak Railway meets the canal. En route, about one mile beyond Whatstandwell, the canal passes through Gregory Tunnel. Walking through the tunnel is optional as there is an alternative path over the top.

The industrial archaeology of High Peak Junction is complex. A spur, known as Nightingale's Canal, led up to mills at Lea Bridge. William Jessop's aqueduct of 1792 carries the canal across the River Derwent. On the right the Leawood Pumping Station, recently restored, was used to raise water from the river into the canal. The section of the canal from here to Cromford has been made navigable again for narrow-boats.

The Cromford and High Peak Railway was constructed in 1825, connecting High Peak Junction with the Peak Forest Canal at Whaley Bridge. The engineer was Josiah Jessop, who built inclines to carry the line over the limestone plateau. The first of these inclines is known as Sheep Pasture Incline, the gradient being about 1 in 9. The engine house has been demolished, but another engine house has been restored at Middleton Top incline near Wirksworth. This railway/canal venture was unsuccessful due to the

LEAWOOD PUMPING STATION

22

WHATSTANDWELL TO BILBERRY KNOLL.

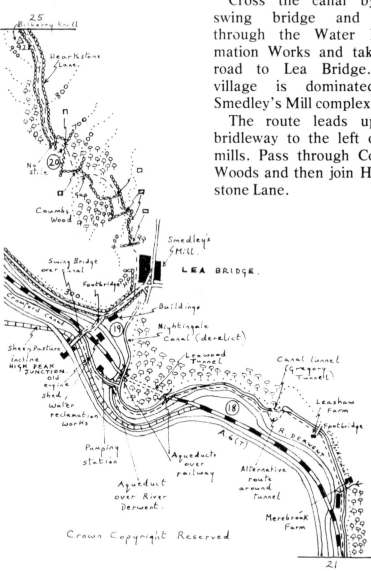

25
Bilberry Knoll
92
Hearthstone Lane.

800

No
stile
20

Coombs
Wood

Swing Bridge
over canal

Footbridge

Cromford Canal

Sheep Pasture
incline
HIGH PEAK
JUNCTION.
old
engine
shed,
water
reclamation
works

Pumping
station

Aqueduct
over River
Derwent.

Smedley's
Mill.

LEA BRIDGE.

Buildings

19

Nightingale
Canal (derelict)

Leawood
Tunnel

18

Aqueducts
over
railway

Canal tunnel
(Gregory
Tunnel)

Leashaw
Farm

Footbridge

R. DERWENT

A.6 (T)

Alternative
route
around
tunnel

Merebrook
Farm

Crown Copyright Reserved

21

advent of other railways, which made the canal section unprofitable. The railway was closed in the 1950s and Derbyshire County Council have converted the route into the High Peak Trail.

Cross the canal by the swing bridge and pass through the Water Reclamation Works and take the road to Lea Bridge. The village is dominated by Smedley's Mill complex.

The route leads up the bridleway to the left of the mills. Pass through Coombs Woods and then join Hearthstone Lane.

BILBERRY KNOLL—CUCKOOSTONE LANE

On reaching Bilberry Knoll make for Riber Castle, a nineteenth century folly built for John Smedley as a residence. After his death it became a school, then a food store and is now a zoo.

The Matlocks may warrant a diversion. Lying in a limestone gorge hewn out by the River Derwent, they are popular with tourists. The area is famous for its caves and lead mining, and Matlock Bath is now the home of Peak District Mining Museum.

RIBER CASTLE

ARKWRIGHT'S MILL, CROMFORD

Further south lies Cromford, the site of several early cotton mills. The Masson Mill on the A6 was built by Richard Arkwright in 1783. The Arkwright Mill of 1772 is situated opposite the Cromford Meadows. Arkwright was also responsible for the industrial housing in North Street and the Greyhound Inn.

The route passes Riber Hall, an early seventeenth century house. Just beyond, a footpath leads across fields to Tansley Knoll. Take

Whitelea Lane out of the village and after about half-a-mile turn left and follow the ridge along Knabhall Lane. Then continue past Packhorse Farm and across fields to Wayside Farm to join Cuckoostone Lane.

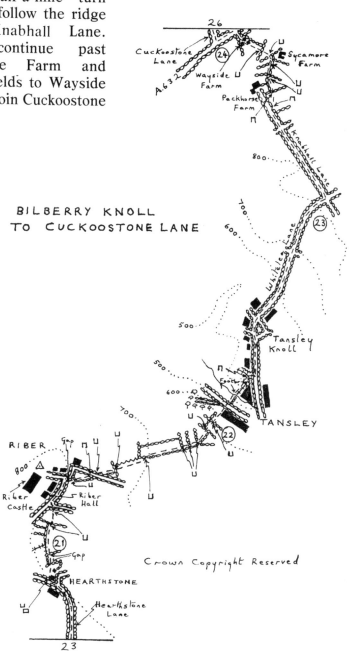

BILBERRY KNOLL
TO CUCKOOSTONE LANE

25

CUCKOOSTONE LANE—GR 300658

The next few miles are rather bleak and make a contrast with the gentle green meadows around Chatsworth which follow. Continue past the end of the wood and cross the fields in a NNE direction.

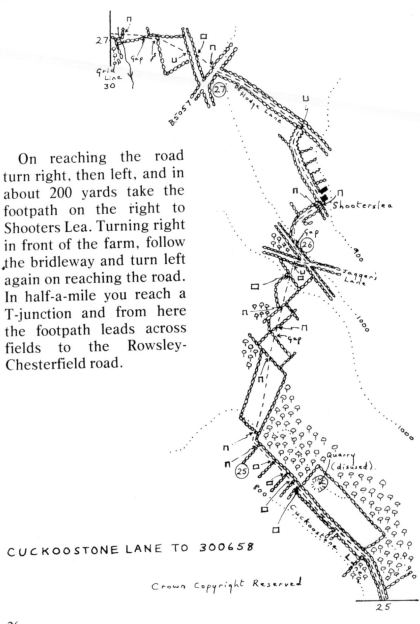

On reaching the road turn right, then left, and in about 200 yards take the footpath on the right to Shooters Lea. Turning right in front of the farm, follow the bridleway and turn left again on reaching the road. In half-a-mile you reach a T-junction and from here the footpath leads across fields to the Rowsley-Chesterfield road.

CUCKOOSTONE LANE TO 300658

26

GR 300658—CHATSWORTH PARK

Follow the Rowsley road downhill for just over a mile, and take the bridleway on the right through Rowsley Wood. In about 350 yards take the indistinct track to the left. When you reach the edge of the wood bear right uphill towards the small footbridge over a stream. Cross it and pass the quarries and follow the tracks downhill towards Beeley.

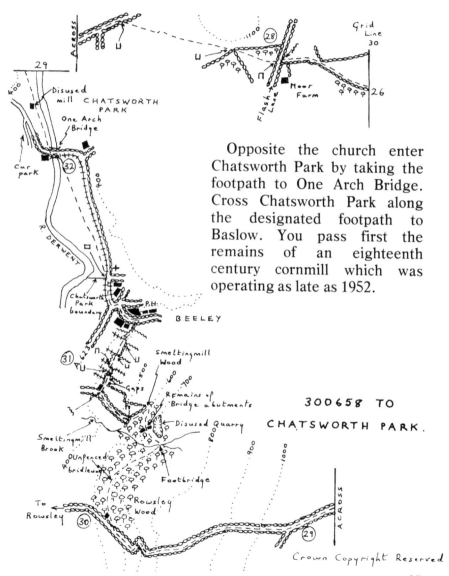

Opposite the church enter Chatsworth Park by taking the footpath to One Arch Bridge. Cross Chatsworth Park along the designated footpath to Baslow. You pass first the remains of an eighteenth century cornmill which was operating as late as 1952.

300658 TO CHATSWORTH PARK.

CHATSWORTH PARK—CURBAR EDGE

Now Chatsworth House may be seen. Sir William Cavendish and his wife, Bess of Hardwick, built the house on this site in the sixteenth century. The present structure was started by the Fourth Earl of Devonshire in 1687 and was extended by his heirs. The grounds were landscaped in the 1760s by 'Capability' Brown. The House and gardens are open to the public during much of the year.

Between 1838-42 the village of Edensor was resited out of view from the House under the direction of the Sixth Duke.

The only surviving portions of the original tudor establishment are the Hunting Tower and Queen Mary's Bower. The former can be seen on the hillside overlooking the House. Queen Mary's Bower lies on our route and is reputed to have been used by Mary, Queen of Scots, during her periods of captivity at Chatsworth.

For those interested in Stately Homes, Haddon Hall is only a few miles away between Rowsley and Bakewell. Most of the structure dates from the fifteenth century. The hall is the home of the Duke of Rutland and is open to the public during the summer.

THE BRIDGE, CHATSWORTH

28

CHATSWORTH TO CURBAR EDGE.

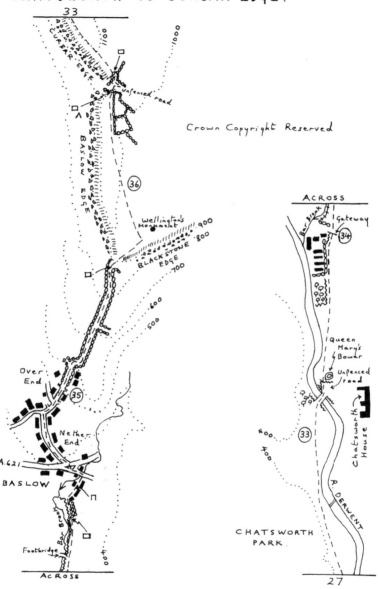

33

CURBAR EDGE

BASLOW EDGE

Unfenced road

36

Wellington's Monument

BLACKSTONE EDGE

900
800
700
600
500

Over End

35

Nether End

A.621

BASLOW

Bar Brook

Footbridge

400

Across

ACROSS

Bar Brook

Gateway

34

Queen Mary's Bower

Unfenced road

Chatsworth House

33

400
400

CHATSWORTH PARK.

R. DERWENT

27

29

The picturesque village of Baslow lies on the River Derwent. By the seventeenth century bridge can be seen a small toll-house. The village church is worth visiting to see the Saxon coffin stone, now part of the porch, and the clock-face with letters reading 'VICTORIA 1897'.

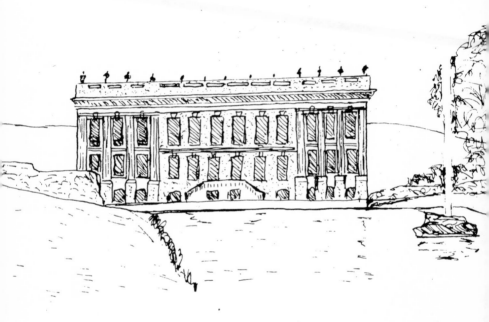

CHATSWORTH HOUSE

At Baslow, go up Eaton Hill, then turn right up the lane to Wellington's Monument, constructed in 1866 by E.M. Wrench as a memorial to the Iron Duke. At this point Nelson's Monument can be seen at Birchen Edge about a mile away.

HADDON HALL

From Wellington's Monument the route follows Derbyshire's eastern gritstone edges — Baslow, Curbar, Froggatt, Burbage and Stanage—names well known in British climbing circles.

WELLINGTON'S MONUMENT

CURBAR EDGE—UPPER PADLEY

By the path a Froggatt Edge there is a Bronze Age stone circle. Shortly beyond this, descend to Grindleford Station where there is a small café. The entrance to the 3½ mile long Totley Railway tunnel built in 1893 can be seen from here.

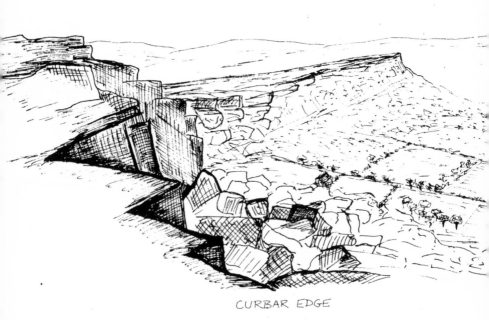

CURBAR EDGE

CURBAR EDGE TO UPPER PADLEY.

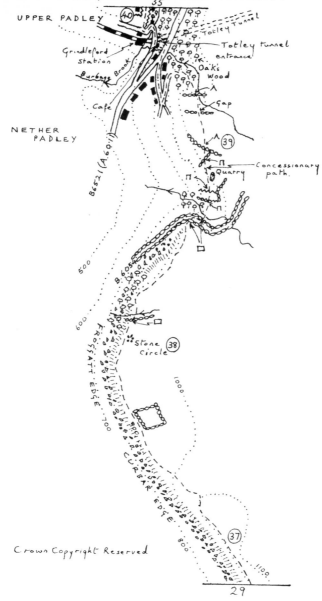

UPPER PADLEY

Grindleford station

Burbage Brook

Café

NETHER PADLEY

B6521 (A.6011)

Totley Tunnel

Totley tunnel entrance

Oak's Wood

Gap

Concessionary path.

Quarry

500

600

FROGGATT EDGE

700

Stone Circle

CURBAR EDGE

800

1000

1100

33

UPPER PADLEY—STANAGE EDGE

The route now passes up Padley Gorge, a relic oak woodland noted for its bird-life, especially pied flycatchers. These are summer visitors and several pairs breed in the nest boxes provided. A publication on the nature trail is available from the Peak Park Planning Board.

Emerging from the woodland, continue along Burbage Brook. On the right one can see Longshaw Lodge, formerly the property of the Duke of Rutland and now owned by the National Trust.

Cross the footbridge before the road and continue to the car park. Take the path leading to the top of Burbage Edge. The section from here to Upper Burbage Bridge lies just within the Sheffield City boundary and is, therefore, the only part of the walk not in Derbyshire. Remains of the stone-cutting industry can be seen here. A partly cut stone trough and a large mill-stone are visible by the path.

Also along this section in summer may be observed the ring ouzel—the 'mountain' version of the blackbird. On the opposite side of the valley can be seen Carl Wark, a well-preserved Iron Age hill fort.

Keep on the top of the edge to Upper Burbage Bridge. Make for Stanage Edge across the Access Land.

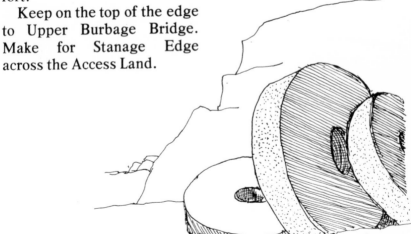

UNFINISHED MILLSTONES, BURBAGE EDGE

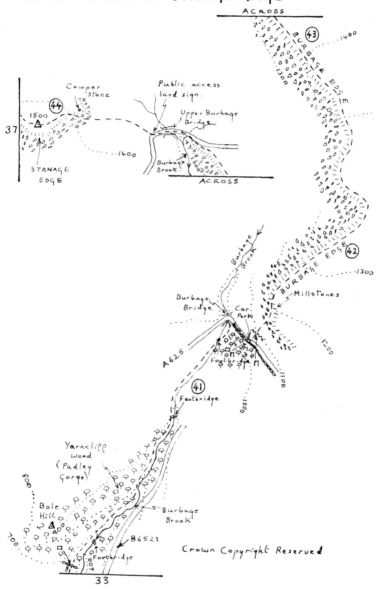

ACROSS

ACROSS

43

1400

Cowper stone

Public access land sign.

44

1500

Upper Burbage Bridge

37

1400

STANAGE EDGE

Burbage Brook

ACROSS

Burbage Brook

42

1300

Millstones

1200

Burbage Bridge

Car Park

A625

Footbridge

1100

41

Footbridge

1000

Yarncliff Wood (Padley Gorge)

Burbage Brook

800

Bole Hill

B6521

Crown Copyright Reserved

700

Footbridge

33

35

STANAGE EDGE—YORKSHIRE BRIDGE

Stanage Edge offers extensive views of the surrounding countryside. In the valley towards Hathersage lies North Lees Hall, a sixteenth century manor house. The story goes that Robert Eyre, who lived at Highlow Hall, had seven sons. He supervised the construction of houses for them within sighting distance, so that signals could be used for communication. North Lees Hall is one of the seven, and is thought to be the setting of Marsh End in Jane Eyre by Charlotte Bronte.

Hathersage churchyard is reputed to be the burial place of Little John and a cave known as Robin Hood's Cave is situated half-way up Stanage Edge.

Leave Stanage Edge by the track leading to Dennis Knoll and take the lane to Yorkshire Bridge.

STANAGE EDGE

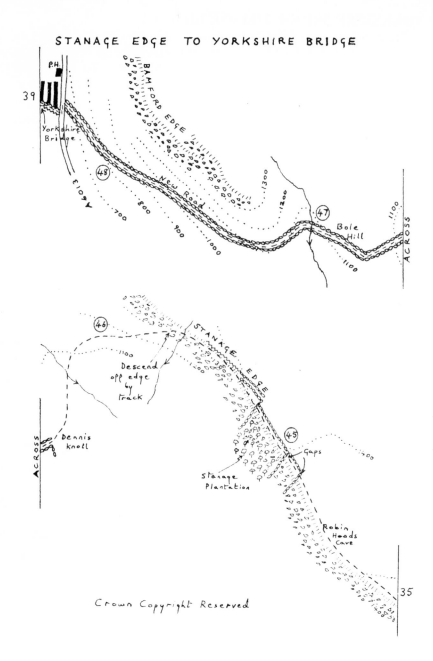

Crown Copyright Reserved

37

YORKSHIRE BRIDGE TO LOSE HILL

Prepare yourself for a very steep climb up Parkin Clough to the summit of Win Hill Pike. This unusual shaped hill, looking somewhat like a volcano, affords superb vistas. To the north lie the Ladybower, Derwent and Howden Reservoirs. These are the impoundments which supply water to parts of the East Midlands, the line of the aqueduct being in evidence during much of the walk.

Leave Win Hill, passing the now derelict Twitchill Farm and ascend Lose Hill from Townhead Bridge. A viewpoint cairn has been placed on the summit.

LADYBOWER RESERVOIR FROM WIN HILL

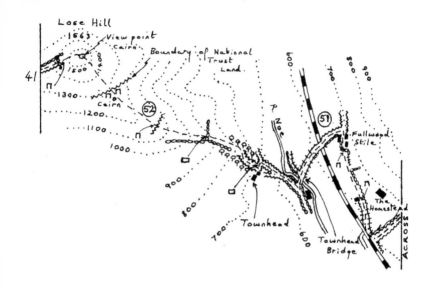

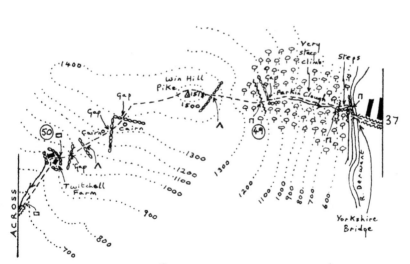

Crown Copyright Reserved.

LOSE HILL—EDALE

The route from Lose Hill to Mam Tor is one of the finest ridge walks in Derbyshire. From the ridge you can see the valley of the River Noe with Edale nestling below Kinder Scout. Continue over Back Tor, where there is a relic of scots pine forest passing Hollins Cross, which is part of an ancient trackway through the col (the lowest point on the ridge). Another viewpoint cairn has been placed here.

We now come to the final climb on the walk (and the highest point)—the summit of Mam Tor. The name Mam Tor is derived from the Celtic, meaning Mother Mountain, and its summit is crowned by an Iron Age hill fort. It is also known as the Shivering Mountain because the face, being composed of alternate layers of sandstone and shale, is susceptible to landslips. Back Tor is also an example of a landslip.

Between Mam Tor and Castleton are several mines in the limestone. They were used for the extraction of galena (lead ore) and the three gangue minerals (fluorspar, barytes and calcite) since Roman times. Now the extractions are limited to the blue or yellow form of fluorspar called Blue John. It is thought that the name Blue John is derived from the French 'bleu et jaune'. Four caverns are open to the public.

From Mam Tor descend to Edale via Greenlands. Fieldhead, the National Park Information Centre, marks the terminal point of the Derbyshire Gritstone way.

Edale is endowed with a café and two hostelries for thirst quenching, and if you wish to do a little more walking, then proceed to Grindsbrook and the start of the Pennine Way.

WIN HILL FROM LOSE HILL

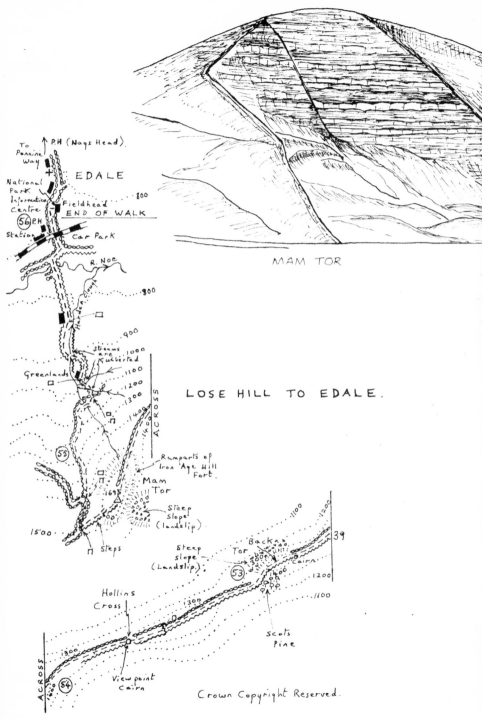

MAM TOR

LOSE HILL TO EDALE.

To Pennine Way

P.H (Nags Head).

EDALE

National Park Information Centre

Fieldhead END OF WALK

(56) P.H

Station

Car Park

R. Noe

800

800

Hollins Clough

900

streams are culverted

1000

Greenlands

1100

1200

1300

1400

(55)

ACROSS

Ramparts of Iron Age Hill Fort.

Mam Tor

1695

Steep Slope (landslip).

1500

Steps

Steep slope (landslip).

Back Tor

(53)

Cairn

1100

1200

39

1100

1200

Hollins Cross

1300

Scots Pine

ACROSS

1300

(54)

Viewpoint Cairn

Crown Copyright Reserved.

41

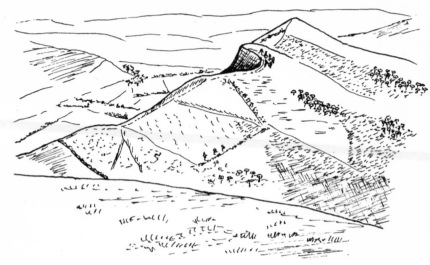

BACK TOR — LOSE HILL RIDGE FROM MAM TOR

EDALE FROM MAM TOR

LIST OF ACCOMMODATION

1. CAMPSITES

Whatstandwell GR 330541	Haytop Farm Ambergate 2063
Whatstandwell GR 330550	Merebrook Caravan Company Ambergate 2154
Matlock Moor GR 321620	Wayside Farm Matlock 2967
Matlock Moor GR 323617	Packhorse Farm Matlock 2781
Baslow GR 275726	Eric Byne Memorial Campsite Moorside Farm
Edale GR 118849	Waterside Farm Barber Booth
Edale GR 125856	Fieldhead Edale (requires advance booking)
Edale GR 123859	Coopers Camp & Caravan Site Newfold Farm, Edale Hope Valley 70372

2. YOUTH HOSTELS

Shining Cliff, Ambergate	GR 335522
Matlock Bath	GR 295585
Fly Hill, Bakewell	GR 215686
The Edge, Eyam	GR 219769
Castleton Road, Hathersage	GR 226815
Castleton Hall	GR 150828
Rowland Cote, Nether Booth, Edale	GR 140866

3. BED & BREAKFAST establishments are best identified by consulting either the R.A. Bed & Breakfast Guide or a local Tourist Information Centre.

DERBY

Derby Industrial Museum   Tel: Derby 31111
Open Tuesday—Friday 10.00 to 17.45
Saturdays 10.00 to 16.45
Closed—Mondays, Sundays and Bank Holidays

Derby Museum and Art Gallery   Tel: Derby 31111
Open Tuesday—Friday 10.00 to 18.00
Open Saturdays 10.00 to 17.00
Closed Mondays, Sundays and Bank Holidays

Kedleston Hall (4 miles NW of Derby) Tel: Derby
840396
Open Bank Holidays and Sundays during the summer

CRICH

Crich Tramway Museum   Tel: Ambergate 2565
Open April—October: Saturdays, Sunday and Bank
Holidays 10.30 to 17.30
June—August: Tuesday, Wednesday and Thursday
10.00 to 16.30
Crich Stand—Open daily

CROMFORD

Leawood Pumping Station: Details of open days from
Cromford Canal Society Ltd., Old Wharf, Mill Road,
Cromford.   Tel: Wirksworth 3727

Middleton Top Engine House. Tel: Wirksworth 3204
Open Sundays. In steam first Saturday in each month

MATLOCK

Peak District Mining Museum   Tel: Matlock 3835
Open daily

Heights of Abraham   Tel: Matlock 2365
Open daily

Riber Castle (Zoo)   Tel: Matlock 2073
Open daily

Great Rutland Cavern
Open daily Easter to October: 100.00 to 18.00

Great Masson Cavern
Open Sundays and Bank Holidays Easter to October
and daily in August: 11.00 to 18.00

BAKEWELL	Old House Museum	Tel: **Bakewell 3647**
	Open daily Easter to October: 14.30 to 17.00	
	Haddon Hall	Tel: **Bakewell 2855**
	Open April to September, Tuesdays to Saturdays and Bank Holidays: 11.00 to 18.00	
BASLOW	Chatsworth House	Tel: **Baslow 2204**
	Open April to October most days	
CASTLETON	Peveril Castle	
	Open daily	
	Blue John Cavern	Tel: **Hope Valley 20642**
	Open daily: 09.30 to 18.00	
	Peak Cavern	Tel: **Hope Valley 20285**
	Open daily Easter to mid-September 10.00 to 18.00	
	Speedwell Cavern	Tel: **Hope Valley 20512**
	Open daily from 09.30	
	Treak Cliff Cavern	Tel: **Hope Valley 20571**
	Open daily from 10.00	

GRINDSBROOK LOOKING TOWARDS KINDER SCOUT

USEFUL NAMES & ADDRESSES

Peak Park Information Centre
Fieldhead
Edale
Nr Sheffield

Trent Motor Traction
National Bus Co.
Uttoxeter Road
Derby

Peak National Park Information Centre
Market Hall, Bridge Street,
Bakewell, Derbyshire

Tourist Information Centre
The Strand
Derby

Peak Park Planning Board
Aldern House
Bakewell, Derbyshire

Tourist Information Centre
The Pavilion
Matlock Bath

Youth Hostels Association
Trevelyan House
St. Albans
Herts AL1 2DY

The National Trust
PO Box 30
Beckenham
Kent

THE RAMBLERS' ASSOCIATION

The Ramblers' Association is a national organisation for all those interested in preserving public paths. It has over 30,000 individual members but needs more.

Up and down the country there are now over 160 local groups of the Ramblers' Association. When you become a member, you are eligible to join your local R.A. Group and take part in its activities at no extra subscription. What does a local group do?

It organises a programme of walks and social events for its members.

It looks after the local footpaths by opposing closures unfavourable to ramblers and by helping to keep paths waymarked and clear of overgrowth.

R.A. membership is open to all. Full details can be obtained from The Ramblers' Association, 1/5 Wandsworth Road, London SW8 2LJ

THE COUNTRY CODE

Enjoy the countryside and respect its life and work
Guard against all risk of fire
Fasten all gates
Keep dogs under close control
Keep to public paths across farmland
Use gates and stiles to cross fences, hedges and walls
Leave livestock, crops and machinery alone
Take your litter home
Help to keep all water clean
Conserve wildlife, plants and trees
Take special care on country roads
Make as little noise as you can

KEY TO SYMBOLS ON MAPS.

Map Scale $2\frac{1}{2}'' = 1$ ml.
   North is at the Top of every page.

30   The route is indicated by dashed lines.
     The number encircled being mileage
     from Derby.

⑫   Terminating line and number indicate
     page continuation, or "across" means
     continuation on another map on the same
                                    page.

Wall   Fence   Hedge   Trees.

Stream or River
with direction of   Contours at 100'
flow.   intervals.

Railway Line   Buildings.   + Church.

Steep Slopes.   △ Triangulation
                      Pillar.

// Road (no information on walls, etc).

□ Gate   ⊔⊓ Stile   Step Stile   ∧ Ladder
                                          Stile.

The maps in this publication are based upon
Ordnance Survey maps with the permission of
the Controller of H.M. Stationary Office.
Crown Copyright reserved.

─────────────────────────

O.S. Maps giving a general coverage
     of the route are :-

1 : 63,360 Peak District Tourist Map.
1 : 50,000 Buxton, Matlock, Dovedale - sheet 119.
1 : 50,000 Derby, Burton-On-Trent - sheet 128.

48